The War Between The States

60 ESSENTIAL BOOKS

The War Between The States

60 ESSENTIAL BOOKS

Clyde N. Wilson

SOUTHERN READER'S GUIDE II

SHOTWELL PUBLISHING
Columbia, SC

Produced in the Republic of South Carolina by

SHOTWELL PUBLISHING, LLC
Post Office Box 2592
Columbia, South Carolina 29202

www.ShotwellPublishing.com

Cover Image: "The Flag of Sumter, Oct. 20, 1863" (1864) by Conrad Wise Chapman
Cover Design: Hazel's Dream | Boo Jackson TCB

ISBN-13: 978-1-947660-17-5
ISBN-10: 1-947660-17-9

10 9 8 7 6 5 4 3 2 1

For Howard White

Extraordinary Colleague in Redeeming the South

Contents

So Southerners are able to know who they are because they have never forgotten what they were.

—Dr. Mark R. Winchell of South Carolina

The South is a garden. It has been worn out by the War, Reconstruction, the Period of Desolation, the Depression and the worst ravages of all—Modernity; yet, a worn-out garden, its contours perceived by keen eyes, the fruitfulness of its past stored in memory, can be over time, a time which will last no longer than those of us who initially set our minds to the task, restored, to once again produce, for the time appointed unto it, the fruits which nurture the human spirit and which foreshadow the Garden of which there will be no end.

—Dr. Robert M. Peters of Louisiana

INTRODUCTION

ALEXANDER STEPHENS INVENTED the term "the War Between the States" as a better description of the conflict of 1861—1865 than "Civil War." He was quite right that it was not a civil war, which is a conflict between two sides over the control of one regime. (Although it sometimes seemed like a "civil war" when it divided families and neighbourhoods.) The U.S. government's term "the War of the Rebellion," is self-righteously fraudulent because no one thought of secession as "rebellion" before Lincoln, cunningly and presumptuously magisterial, declared it so. The Southern States only wanted their traditional self-government while elements of the Northern States, in control of the central state machinery, wanted to control all the people, territory, and resources. A precisely accurate term is offered by Dr. Charles T. Pace: "The War to Prevent Southern Independence."

Whatever we call it, the war is still the biggest thing in American history in the scale of mobilization and casualties, in the drama of great events, in the glamour of great personalities, in imposed revolutionary change of the American regime, and in the powerful melodramatic myth of special American righteousness. The immense happening created a vast literature than can never be mastered in one lifetime.

The selections here are primarily designed to lead the reader to works that are informative, enjoyable, and reflective of the heroism and sacrifice of the Confederate people. It is hoped that the selections herein will guide readers to even more good works.

This work began as a guide to books that tell the true history of the Confederacy. But given the pervasive and malicious campaign against everything Southern that marks our time, I decided to add some titles that question the myths of Northern and Lincolnian righteousness. This Northern mythology is far less truthful and far more dangerous than "the Lost Cause Myth" that historians are at the moment attacking. I knew a historian who had studied with Douglas Southall Freeman. He told the story that Freeman was once asked: "Now that you have done the history of the Army of Northern Virginia, why don't you write the history of the opposing Northern army?" Freeman replied, "I can't do it. There is too much ugliness in that army."

As in the predecessor work, *The Old South: 50 Essential Books*, the recommendations include both history and creative literature. Unless there is some forbidding accident there will be third volume about "Reconstruction" and the following "New South" period, and a fourth about the 20th century and beyond. The guide in hand concentrates on the War itself rather than the unfortunate lasting consequences of how it turned out.

There is no particular significance in the order in which titles are presented. They come just as they occurred to the author. Of course, in a literature so vast we have doubtless missed many readers' favourites. But the suggestions herein include many substantial and indispensable works as well as some overlooked treasures. Please let me know of any especially good titles I may have missed at Shotwell@sc.rr.com.

Note that many of our selections are from the period and written by participants in the time. Among other things, such works are a useful corrective to what passes for historical knowledge today. Anybody who actually reads what Jefferson Davis had to say will see at once that much of what is passed around these days about the War Between the States is not knowledge at all—it is merely the pasting on of labels by pretended "experts" who don't know what they are talking about. The study of history should be a search for understanding human experience, but for such "experts" it is only an ideological tool for suppression of debate. Not too long-ago historians were trained for painstaking research and valued by their knowledge of "primary sources." Today they are trained and valued for the ability to spout the current party line.

The best work today is being done by non-academic historians.

Except where particularly significant, we have not tried to account for the publishing history or the means of acquiring particular works. Most readers today are familiar with the online acquisition of books, new and old.

Clyde N. Wilson
Dutch Fork, Republic of South Carolina

I. THE CONFEDERACY

Truth crushed to earth is truth still, and like a seed will rise again.
—Jefferson Davis

If the rulers in the United States had been good Christian men, the present war would not have come upon us.
—Confederate Schoolbook

1.

The Unvanquished

By William Faulkner

Here is the War Between the States novel of the greatest American writer of the 20th century. It recounts the endurance and courage of three generations of a Mississippi family in the face of overwhelming destruction. The family includes the hero Colonel Sartoris; Grandmother Rosa Millard, a paragon of integrity who yet finds a way to cheat the Yankees and keep the people of Yoknapatawpha County fed; lovely Cousin Drusilla who becomes a soldier; the boys Bayard (white) and Ringo (black) who have to learn to survive a life in wartime. For those who find Faulkner's writing difficult or intimidating, *The Unvanquished* is a good place to begin to understand his genius. (Another good place to start is *Intruder in the Dust,* which takes place in a later period.)

2.

North Against South: The American Iliad, 1848—1877

By Ludwell H. Johnson

This is a book that should be read and re-read and digested by every American who wants to understand the causes, conduct, and results of the War Between the States. Most of the writing and general public knowledge of the central event in American history rests upon a Northern viewpoint—the South is to be understood as provoking war by resistance to a benevolent government in unforgivable defense of slavery. Written with strict professional historianship and superb mastery of the sources and literature, *North Against South* tells a different story—not by defending the South but by close examination of the motives and actions of the North. Ludwell Johnson was a Virginian with a Ph.D. from Johns Hopkins University and a long-time popular professor of history at William and Mary College. The book originally appeared under the title *Division and Reunion: America, 1844—1877*. Besides this book, Johnson left excellent articles scattered through many publications which urgently need to be gathered and published: "The Plundering Generation" (Republicans in the War era), on Lincoln mythology, on Lee's critics, on Ken Burns' television atrocity, and an interesting article about how the U.S. Supreme Court in post-war litigation was forced to admit that the Confederacy had been a legitimate government.

3.

The Story of the Confederacy
By Robert Selph Henry

Robert Selph Henry (1889—1970) was a Tennessean, a World War I soldier, a railroad executive, and the best sort of non-professional historian. His straightforward telling of Confederate history is good as a general work and as a starting place for beginners in War Between the States study. Henry also wrote *The Story of Reconstruction, The Story of the Mexican War,* and *"First With the Most"*—*General Nathan Bedford Forrest.* Besides that biography, one of the best on Forrest, Henry edited an excellent collection of first-hand accounts of the "Wizard of the Saddle"— *As They Saw Forrest.*

4.

Jefferson Davis: Essential Writings
Edited by William J. Cooper

This well-made collection contains our President's major speeches and public papers and a generous selection of his letters. Integrity, eloquence, and high-order statesmanship shine through all of Davis's words. They may be favourably compared to a similar collection of the writings of Lincoln or any other Northern leader. Don't, however, neglect the fine biographies by Hudson Strode, Elizabeth Allen, and Mrs. Varina (Howell) Davis.

5.

Traveller

By Richard Adams

Richard Adams, the English author of the classic allegorical tale *Watership Down*, conceived a unique way to tell the story of the War for Southern Independence — through the eyes of General R.E. Lee's famous horse Traveller. After all, Traveller was present at almost all of the great battles of the Army of Northern Virginia and in daily close contact with its commander. As a horse he, of course, did not understand everything, but he was shrewd about what he observed first-hand. Interestingly, Traveler thought we had won the war since the Yankees stopped attacking and he and his master retired to a quiet life. Like Granny Clampett of "The Beverly Hillbillies," he felt that it was natural that the Americans won in the war between the Yankees and the Americans. There is a particularly egregious Yankee historian who whines that nobody ever wrote a book about Grant's horse.

6.

A History of the Confederate Navy

By Raimondo Luraghi

Professor Luraghi of the University of Genoa has been recognised as the leading European historian of the American War Between the States. This scholarly and well-written history contains everything you want to know about Confederate naval affairs— the Navy Department, the building yards, on the inland waters, around the seaports, and on the high seas. It is a story of how supposedly backward Southerners performed remarkable feats of ingenuity and enterprise in building a navy almost from scratch. (Luraghi is also author of a general history of The War that, alas, has never been translated from the Italian.)

7.

The Confederate War

By Gary W. Gallagher

This 1997 work analyses the experience of the Southern people in the great War for Independence. It becomes clear that, despite what some commentators have alleged, the Confederacy was very much supported by the Southern people, whose extraordinary courage, devotion, and sacrifice has never been equaled by any large group of

Americans. Interestingly, in his first two books, this and a biography of General Stephen D. Ramseur, Professor Gallagher, born in California, was a fair-minded historian of the South. In his later works, he has succumbed to the academically respectable anti-South consensus.

8.

The Fremantle Diary: Being the Journal of Lieutenant Colonel Arthur James Lyon Fremantle, Coldstream Guards, on His Three Months in the Southern States

This is a vital Confederate document. Col. Fremantle entered the Confederacy in March 1863 at Brownsville, Texas, at the mouth of the Rio Grande, traveled overland to Virginia, and accompanied the Army of Northern Virginia to Gettysburg. He had ample opportunity to observe Southern soldiers and civilians. He came with a feeling of indifference about the two sides in the war, but "soon a sentiment of great admiration for the gallantry and determination of the Southerners" caused a complete change in his feelings. Fremantle wrote that "no generous man, whatever may be his political opinions, can do otherwise than admire the courage, energy, and patriotism of the whole population, and the skill of its leaders, in this struggle against great odds." I do not think that Fremantle, by the way, was very well portrayed in the "Gettysburg" film.

9.

The Civil War: A Narrative (3 vols.)

By Shelby Foote

No reading recommendation on the War Between the States can omit Shelby Foote's epic narrative. Strictly as narrative it is the best thing ever written or that ever will be written on the subject. Foote tells *the story* of the great event comprehensively and in beautiful style. One does not read about the battle of Gettysburg, one feels it coming on and lives it. Every area is given full attention— the east, the middle theatre, and the Trans-Mississippi. The great characters of this great period of history are portrayed with realism and depth. Clearly Foote's favourite characters are those with connection to his native Mississippi—Jefferson Davis and Bedford Forrest, but his treatment of Northern people like Lincoln and Grant is also sympathetic and insightful.

Foote (1916—2005) began as a novelist but devoted 20 years to producing this history, which I dare to suggest will be as nearly immortal as any book can be. The author served in World War II and his work reflects the nationalism of that period. Like many Southerners of the time he viewed the war as a great tragedy but which brought about a stronger and better nation. When the last space ship departs this exploding earth, this work should be on it.

10.

The Long Roll (1911) and *Cease Firing* (1912)
By Mary Johnston

Mary Johnston (1870—1936) was a best-selling novelist of the early 20th century and had three of her books made into movies. She was a Virginian, notably progressive for her time, and a niece of General Joe Johnston. These stories of Virginian men and women suffering through the ravages of invasion are sympathetic and at the same time realistic and unsentimental. Mary Johnston is a writer who has unjustly fallen out of notice.

11.

So Good a Cause: A Decade of Southern Partisan
Edited by Oran P. Smith

This collection contains material from the best years of the now defunct *Southern Partisan*, 1983—1993. Where else can you find such gems as M.E. Bradford on the theology of secession, Russell Kirk on Randolph and Calhoun, two essays by Richard Weaver, "The Quotable Robert E. Lee" by Rod Gragg, "The Plundering Generation" and "PBS's 'The Civil War': The Mythmanagement of History" by Ludwell H. Johnson, Thomas Landess on "the Dark Side of Abraham Lincoln," Forrest McDonald on "Why Yankees Won't (and Can't) Leave the South Alone," J.O. Tate on the slandering of General Forrest, and much else. A collection well worth savouring.

12.

Lone Star Preacher

By John W. Thomason

Thomason (1893—1944), a native Texan, was at the same time a talented and prolific writer/artist and a serving Marine Corps officer. In World War I he received the Navy Cross, the Navy's highest award for bravery, and he is probably the only writer who has had a U.S. Navy destroyer named for him. *Lone Star Preacher* is a delightful account of the adventures of the Rev. Mr. Praxiteles Swan. Swan was an early settler on the Texas frontier, was called to the ministry of the Methodist Church, and was a chaplain and then a combat officer with the famous Texas Brigade of the Army of Northern Virginia. Thomason had a good ear for Southern speech and a good feel for Southern attitudes. This is one of my favourite books.

Thomason also wrote, among other works, a biography of Jeb Stuart and two once very popular collections of stories on Marines in World War I and on the Chinese station—*Fix Bayonets!* and—*And a Few Marines.*

13.

The South Was Right!

By James Ronald Kennedy & Walter Donald Kennedy

This best-selling instant classic in 1994 created an avalanche of renewed interest among War Between the States readers. With evidence and eloquence the authors took apart the Northern mythology that dominates discussion of the war and reaffirmed the essential soundness of the Southern cause. Much renewal of Southern morale and thought is the result. Enough said.

14.

The Valiant Virginians

By James Warner Bellah

James Warner Bellah (1899-1976) was a New York native, journalist, active officer in World War I and World War II, and a prolific author of novels, mostly Westerns. Several of his novels were made into famous John Ford movies, including "Fort Apache," "She Wore a Yellow Ribbon," and "Rio Grande." He wrote the screenplay for other well-known Western movies. Bellah always had sympathy and respect for Confederates. This book is a delightful series of stories about three Virginians who were "out with Jackson" for the duration of the war. The author captures the speech and attitudes of Southerners well and sympathetically. One of my favourites.

15.

Memoirs of Service Afloat, During the War Between the States
By Raphael Semmes

I rank this, along with Richard Taylor's, as the best of Confederate memoirs. Semmes was a very good writer, with an acerbic wit for Yankee misbehaviour. His epic voyage around the globe on the high seas in command of the raider *Alabama* literally devastated the Yankee merchant marine. It is worth noting that Semmes, a Maryland Catholic by birth, was, unlike his opponents, always a gentlemen. No sailor on any of the many Yankee ships he captured or destroyed ever suffered harm. Every one was set ashore in a safe location. Any student of Southern history and of the War Between the States will be delighted to get acquainted with the Confederacy's greatest naval hero.

16.

Destruction and Reconstruction: Personal Experiences of the Late War

By Richard Taylor

Richard Taylor was the son of President Zachary Taylor and the brother-in-law of President Jefferson Davis. He was a well-educated and well-read man who was living quietly on his Louisiana plantation when the War Between the States approached. Not a professional soldier, he became an outstanding Confederate general. In 1864 in the Red River campaign he defeated and sent running a much larger federal force supported by gunboats. (Of course, despite being shamefully defeated by Taylor's small force, the invasion achieved its goal: General Banks and Admiral Porter became rich men on stolen cotton.)

Taylor was a good writer and perceptive man who moved in high circles and knew almost everybody of importance on both sides. Among many other insights and incidents he tells of Stonewall Jackson gently reprimanding him for cursing in battle; of how the educated Taylor and the rough-hewn Forrest hit it off immediately; and assesses probably as well as has ever been done the reasons why Braxton Bragg failed. I will have to call this the best of all Confederate memoirs. The 1998 republication has an introduction by Yours Truly.

17.

Understanding the War Between the States

Edited by Howard R. White and Clyde N. Wilson

Sixteen scholars of the Society of Independent Southern Historians provide 40 concise chapters that tell the facts of the great conflict —from the antagonistic cultures of New England and Virginia in the 1600s to the end of "Reconstruction." This work is designed for classroom discussions or for the enlightenment of anyone from bright high school student on up. Any Southerner who knows this work need never lose an argument with an advocate of the Northern version of The War. It is available in bulk at cost from SouthernHistorians.org, which website also contains a very large catalogue of books on Southern history and culture.

18.

When the Yankees Come: Former South Carolina Slaves Remember Sherman's Invasion

Edited by Paul C. Graham

One imagines that many Americans visualise Sherman's heroic boys in blue as they advanced through the South being greeted by joyous, newly emancipated African Americans. Nothing could be further from the truth. Most Union soldiers cared nothing for black people and considered them either as prey or a nuisance. The boys in blue as readily or more readily robbed and abused black Southerners than they did white. Most renderings of such encounters neglect to mention that when housing, food, and the means of making a living are destroyed by an invading army, the black people are left starving and homeless as well as the white. Graham has dared to look at what black survivors actually had to say about such encounters. On the whole it was not a pleasant experience. Recollections are from the *Slave Narratives* recorded in the 1930s. They have often been criticized but they are shrewd and generally consistent in their accounts.

19.

Gone With the Wind (1936)

by Margaret Mitchell

Of course, no Southern list of books on The War can overlook this Southern icon. There is a familiar story that the author had stuffed her couch with the unsold manuscript. When a New York literary agent visited Atlanta she got it out. The result was in its time *the* top international best-seller, translated into every language in which books were printed, and turned into an all-time blockbuster movie. Although *Gone With the Wind* has some soap opera elements, it is also a true picture of what

Southerners suffered in The War and "Reconstruction," just as the author intended. Re-reading the work after some years, I gained an increased respect for its literary quality, an experience in which I am not alone. I suggest that serious readers follow up *GWTW* with *None Shall Look Back*, by the great novelist Caroline Gordon, published about the same time and with a similar theme, but with a more highbrow treatment.

20.

With Blood and Fire: Life Behind Union Lines in Middle Tennessee, 1863-65

By Michael R. Bradley

It has long been recognized among civilised governments than when a territory is conquered or surrendered, the occupying power assumes responsibility for law and order, for the protection of civil society. The U.S. Army in The War paid no attention to civilised understanding in its invasion campaigns directed chiefly at civilians, nor in the areas of the South that it successfully occupied. Instead it engaged in murder, authorized and unauthorized, unjust imprisonments, seizing of innocent hostages, wholesale robbery and destruction of property. Professor Bradley of Tennessee has marshaled the telling ugly evidence of this "Unknown Battlefield" for one area of the occupied South. The same could be done for every other occupied area.

21.

Macaria, or Altars of Sacrifice (1864)

By Augusta Jane Evans

This book sold 20,000 copies in the beleaguered Confederacy and sold well in a Northern edition as well. Copies found in the possession of Northern soldiers were confiscated and destroyed. *Macaria* tells the experiences of a strong Southern woman in war. Augusta Jane Evans (Mrs. Lorenzo M. Wilson, 1835—1909), of Mobile, Alabama, Confederate nurse, was one of the most successful American writers of the 19th century. Her *St. Elmo*, published the year after the War Between the States, was an international best-seller, rivaling *Uncle Tom's Cabin* and *Ben-Hur*. It was produced on the stage a number of times and became a silent film. Its title became literally a household word. Contrary to the "mainstream" interpretation of antebellum Southern women as lightweights in intellect and character, Evans and her characters were strong, intelligent women struggling with questions of faith and their role in society. And also strong Southern patriots. Her novel *Beulah*, published in 1859, gives a similar treatment to the antebellum South. Evans is a gifted writer deserving to be much better known. For the most recent republication of *Macaria* you can safely ignore the Introduction by D.G. Faust, president of Harvard.

22.

R.E. Lee: A Biography (4 vols.)
By Douglas Southall Freeman

This classic is an exhaustive life of one of the greatest Americans and an outstanding exhibit of the biographer's craft. Freeman (1886—1953) was among the foremost historians of the War Between the States in his time and since. He was chosen to show Winston Churchill and Dwight Eisenhower around the Gettysburg battlefield. Though he had a Ph.D. from Johns Hopkins, Freeman, son of a Virginia Confederate soldier, was a newspaper editor and produced his work outside of the academy. Readers of *R.E. Lee* will want to continue with *Lee's Lieutenants: A Study in Command* , 3 vols., published during World War II when military studies were important and Southerners were needed and temporarily in favour. Freeman's *The South to Posterity: An Introduction to the Writing of Confederate History* (1939) is a good guide to what was written by Southern participants in The War. In regard to Lee's place in world military history: with a little work online you can find a 62-page article by British Field Marshal Garnet Wolseley on Lee's generalship.

23.

Recollections Gay and Grave (1911)

By Constance Cary Harrison

This is among the finest of Confederate personal memoirs. Constance Cary (1843—1920) moved in high circles in Richmond during The War. Shortly after, she married Burton Harrison, President Davis's private secretary, as soon as he was released from prison. Interestingly, Mr. and Mrs. Harrison moved to New York City, where he became a prominent public figure and she a prolific and popular writer. I tend to prefer this memoir to the more celebrated "diary" of Mary Boykin Chestnut on war-time Richmond. Mrs. Chestnut's work is quite valuable but it is not really a diary. It is a memoir rewritten from her diary after the war by a woman exercising her literary talent.

24.

Merchant of Terror:
General Sherman and Total War

By John Bennett Walters

This is both a biography of a strange, warped man who commanded an American army and an account of how he pioneered a policy of war that revoked the civilisational progress that had been achieved up to his time. The author, a professor at Montevallo University, writes calmly and factually, allowing Sherman to be convicted by his own words. His policy was to avoid fighting the armed enemy and lead an army on a wide swath through undefended territory, destroying the food and shelter of and humiliating women and children (and black people). For some reason this has led to Sherman being hailed as a great general, although he had been a failure in life until raised up and turned loose by Lincoln and Grant. Sherman embodied the very worst characteristics of the abstract fanaticism of his Connecticut Puritan forebears combined with the shallow intellect and opportunism of his Ohio upbringing. We should never forget that this man could have had the Republican Presidential nomination if he had wanted it.

25.

Reminiscences of Peace and War (1905)

By Mrs. Roger A. Pryor

Sara Agnes Rice (1830—1912) married Roger A. Pryor, Congressman, diplomat, and Confederate brigadier. This is the recollection of a brave and intelligent Southern woman who experienced many of the hardships of war. In the earlier part of The War she accompanied her husband's command and served as a nurse. In the later part she lived with her children in the difficulties of besieged Petersburg. Interestingly, the Pryors after the war moved to New York City where he became a prominent newspaper editor and judge and she a popular writer. Similar to the experience of the Burton Harrisons cited in entry No. 23 herein.

26.

Outlines from the Outpost
By John Esten Cooke

John Esten Cooke (1830—1886) of Virginia was already the author of two successful novels before the War for Southern Independence, and continued that career afterward. During the war he rode with General Jeb Stuart as a staff officer and after Stuart's death served on the staff of General Pendleton, artillery chief of the Army of Northern Virginia. He lived the war in Virginia first-hand. His memoir *Wearing of the Gray* is well-known. But *Outlines*, partly written during or just after the war, is less well-known but perhaps more interesting. Some of these writings about his vivid experiences were published in periodicals during the war. Others were left in manuscript for a book never published. The whole was not collected and published in book form until 1961.

27.

Is Davis a Traitor; Or Was Secession a Constitutional Right Previous to the War of 1861? (1866)

By Albert Taylor Bledsoe

Kentucky native Bledsoe (1809—1877) was a brilliant polymath—mathematician, philosopher, theologian, soldier, professor, clergyman, and editor. In this work Bledsoe takes on all the major commentators against the right of secession and demolishes them irrefutably. The book should be on the shelf of everybody interested in The War. Bledsoe does in 263 pages what Vice-President Alexander H. Stephens does more elaborately in the thick two volumes of *A Constitutional View of the War Between the States.* In 1863 Bledsoe was sent to Europe as a Confederate spokesman. He wrote some of this book in the British Museum library, probably at the same time Karl Marx was scribbling his destructive works in the same place. When he returned to the conquered South Bledsoe was told by General Lee that the Confederacy relied on him for vindication. The author closes the preface to his book thus: "The calm and impartial reader will, it is believed, discover the grounds on which the South may be vindicated, and the final verdict of History determined in favor of a gallant, but down-trodden and oppressed, *PEOPLE.*"

28.

Life and Campaigns of Lieut.-Gen. Thomas J. Jackson (1866)

By Robert Lewis Dabney

To this day Dabney (1820—1898) is recognised as a brilliant Presbyterian theologian. He was a friend of Stonewall Jackson and served for a time on Jackson's staff. Perhaps no one understood Jackson's motives and actions in the war better. The author remarked that, although Jackson's cause was overturned, his fame was permanent. Dabney was one of the brightest, most eloquent and persistent defenders of the South in his prolific writings after the War Between the States. Southern readers should become familiar with his *A Defence of Virginia, and Through Her of the South*, published the year after Jackson's biography. For a more recent Jackson biography, many readers think well of that by James I. Robertson.

29.

Patriotic Gore: Studies in the Literature of the American Civil War

By Edmund Wilson

Wilson, a New Yorker, was considered the most influential American literary critic of his day. He wrote prolifically on a wide variety of subjects. During the Civil War Centennial (1962) he published this book on the writings of participants in The War. It may be that he was moved toward this subject by difficulties with the federal government over tax matters. The title, of course, comes from James Ryder Randall's Confederate lyrics for "Maryland, My Maryland": "Avenge the patriotic gore that flecked the streets of Baltimore." Wilson deals with both sides and in an original way with information and insights that will be new and stimulating to students. Perhaps the most interesting parts are candid examinations of the writings such strange Northern characters as Harriet Beecher Stowe, Julia Ward Howe, and William T. Sherman.

30.

To Die in Chicago: Confederate Prisoners at Camp Douglas

By George Levy

The story of the brutal POW camp at which thousands of Confederates died unnecessarily while Northerners paid to gawk at them from specially built bleachers. After this book, add *Elmira: Death Camp of the North* by Michael Horigan to your reading list. The death and suffering of Confederate prisoners was a product of deliberate policy on the part of at least some Northern officials and of the Lincoln/ Grant refusal to accept their own men from Confederate prisons even under the most favourable conditions. The suffering and death of Union prisoners in Confederate hands, by contrast, was a product of lack of resources in a country under mass invasion, despite heroic efforts at proper treatment. James Madison Page in *A True Story of Andersonville Prison*, was only one of several POW Union officers who blamed Lincoln's administration for Union deaths and vindicated Confederates.

31.

The Confederate Constitution of 1861: An Inquiry Into American Constitutionalism

By Marshall L. DeRosa

As its title indicates, this classic study is more than an examination of the Confederate Constitution, though it is that. It examines the wise work of our Confederate forefathers in keeping the essence of the U.S. Constitution but improving it in a number of ways. They clarified some things that needed clarification. They provided provisions that prevented the log-rolling plunder of the treasury that Northern rent-seekers have made common practice under the U.S. government (before and during the War and ever since). They improved the office of the Presidency by giving him one six-year term, so he would not be preoccupied with re-election, and gave him a line-item veto. They made it much easier for the people to amend the Constitution. And they acknowledged their submission to Divine Providence. The Confederate Constitution is a fruitful study for those interested in genuine constitutional and democratic government.

32.

War Crimes Against Southern Civilians

By Walter Brian Cisco

The Union's war crimes are among the best documented events in history. They can be proved entirely from Northern sources without touching a single Southern testimony, although there are those who continue to deny or minimize them. They did not consist only of Sherman's notorious depredations in Georgia and the Carolinas, but began in the first days of the war and occurred at every place Northern soldiers went. A great deal has been written on the subject, but a comprehensive survey had long been needed. Cisco has provided this with material from every theatre of the war. This is a lasting classic that was long needed and that should be on every Southern bookshelf. For a good exhibit of the hatred and fanaticism that fueled the war crimes, see Charles A. Jennings, *Cultures in Conflict: The Union Desecration of Southern Churches and Cemeteries.*

33.

Bill Arp, So Called: A Sideshow of the Southern Side of the War

Bill Arp was the pen name of Charles Henry Smith (1826-1903), Georgia planter and Confederate major. From the beginning to the end of the war he wrote very popular newspaper sketches of Southern experiences in the form of letters from "Bill Arp," often laced with humour about the Yankees. In 1866 he got a Northern publisher to issue this collection of his wartime pieces, although he was completely unapologetic about his Southern viewpoint. In later years Smith, as an Atlanta columnist, was reprinted widely and was one of the most popular writers in the South. His writings then had more to do with rural life than the war and were popular with many Northern readers. Mark Twain called Smith one of the few true American humourists.

34.

Shiloh

By Shelby Foote

Before he undertook his epic *The Civil War: A Narrative*, Foote wrote this vivid novel about the untried soldiers on both sides who fought in one of the bloodiest battles of American history. A realistic account by a great writer. It makes the War real like no other fiction that I know. Follow up *Shiloh* with Foote's great WBTS novel *Jordan County*.

35.

Uncle Seth Fought the Yankees
By James Ronald Kennedy

The co-author of the classics *The South Was Right!* and *Punished With Poverty: The Suffering South* has produced this memorable account of great Southern deeds in the War to Prevent Southern Independence. Confederate veteran "Uncle Seth" tells the lads of his kin and neighbourhood over 100 tales of Southern courage and skill in triumphs against great odds and of Yankee misdeeds. Give this to your grandchildren, nieces and nephews, who have been exposed to false teachings in school.

36.

The Immortals: A Story of Love and War
By Karen Stokes

South Carolinian Karen Stokes is a highly productive rising star in Southern literature, both history and fiction. It is difficult to choose one of her books, and my choice should be regarded only as an introduction to her works. A story of two Charlestonians who exemplify the experience of their people in war and "Reconstruction." George Taylor is a Confederate officer who endures battle and the debilitating existence of Yankee POW camps. His beloved, Marguerite Finley, endures raids by enemy cavalry and witnesses the destruction of Columbia. After the war they must struggle to rebuild their health, their fortunes, and their interrupted relationship. Look to your laurels, *Gone With the Wind!* Stokes's other books (history and fiction) include *Faith, Valor, and Devotion; A Confederate Englishman; Honor in the Dust; Days of Destruction; South Carolina Civilians in Sherman's Path; The Immortal 600; The Soldier's Ghost: A Tale of Charleston; Belles: A Carolina Love Story; Confederate South Carolina;* and *Carolina Love Letters.* There are more on the way.

37.
The Army of Tennessee
By Stanley F. Horn

The Confederate army that defended against invasion in the vast region between the Appalachians and the Mississippi River was never as well-led nor as famous as the Army of Northern Virginia. But it had its great battles, its great dramatic episodes of success and failure, and great captains like Forrest, Cleburne, Albert Sidney Johnston, Joe Johnston, and Joe Wheeler. In Horn it found its true historian. Stanley F. Horn (1889—1980) was a Tennessean, editor of a trade magazine for the lumber industry, and another of those excellent nonprofessional historians with which the South has been gifted. His history of the Army of Tennessee is factually solid and comprehensive but also portrays the human experience of its soldiers. Horn published a number of other books, including *The Robert E. Lee Reader*, *The Boy's Book of Robert E. Lee*, *The Invisible Empire* (on the original Ku Klux Klan), and studies of various battles of the army that he knew so well.

38.

The Butcher's Cleaver

By W. Patrick Lang

The plot of this fiction trilogy is a somewhat far-fetched but interesting story about the Confederate Secret Service. (*The Butcher's Cleaver* is followed by *Death Piled Hard* and *Down the Sky*.) But along with that story, the author, a VMI graduate, portrays the War in Virginia very vividly and realistically from the Confederate side. I can find no other author who pictures so convincingly what Confederates, both historical figures and ordinary folks, were like in their thoughts, speech, and actions. The author is a decorated former military intelligence office with expertise on the Middle East. His commentary on U.S. actions in that theatre has been anti-establishment, which may have to do with his non-mainstream view of the heroic Southern struggle for independence. For another recent true-to-history Confederate fiction see Thomas G. Moore, *A Fatal Mercy.*

39.

The Life of General Nathan Bedford Forrest (1899)

By John Allen Wyeth

Wyeth (1845—1922) as a lad was a private in an Alabama cavalry regiment that saw service with John Hunt Morgan and Joseph Wheeler. After the war he became a very prominent surgeon in New York City, founding a medical school and serving a term as president of the American Medical Association. His use of sources was thorough and his writing excellent in this account of Forrest's life and campaigns. Despite all the lies and distortions which have become common "knowledge" about Forrest, we should remember that he was one of the most remarkable men in American history. An untrained officer, outnumbered and out-supplied, he again and again and again defeated and dispersed much larger forces. He was one of those men —courageous, skillful, and undaunted in defense of his people — that in better days of Western civilization became legendary heroes. Forrest, contrary to propaganda, was chivalrous, more so than his opponents. At various times both Lee and Sherman remarked that Forrest was the greatest soldier of The War.

40.

A Rebel Born: A Defense of Nathan Bedford Forrest, Confederate General, American Legend

By Lochlainn Seabrook

Despite all the malicious and dishonest negatives that have been aimed at Forrest, he has attracted many sympathetic biographers. Seabrook's is a good place to start. There are other good works by Wyeth, Robert S. Henry, Andrew Lytle, Jack Hurst, and Samuel W. Mitcham. You may safely avoid the PC biography by Brian Wills which has been aptly described as "the last with the least."

41.

To Live and Die in Dixie: The Struggle Continues

Edited by Frank B. Powell III and R. Michael Givens

This is a stellar collection of fresh essays covering a multitude of subjects about the South before, during, and after the War Between the States. The authors include Donald Livingston, David Aiken, Marshall De Rosa, Karen Stokes, Walter B. Cisco, James and Walter Kennedy, Michael R. Bradley, Boyd Cathey, H.V. Traywick and others. These articles are deeply researched and persuasive.

42.

Sack and Destruction of the City of Columbia, S. C.

(1865)

By William Gilmore Simms

The South's greatest living man of letters of the time was an eyewitness to the federal army's devastation of three-fourths of the beautiful city of Columbia and the sufferings of its people. He made this record as a permanent testimony to that event. At the time General Sherman blamed the fire on retreating Confederate soldiers, although in his memoirs he admitted that was a lie intended to further demoralise South Carolinians. Strangely, there are historians eager for place and Chamber of Commerce flunkeys eager for tourist dollars who continue to state that the origins of the multiple fires are uncertain. Somehow, although Sherman's men burned every place they came across both before and after their stay in Columbia, that particular fire was an accident or caused by Southerners. In fact, the deliberate destruction of Columbia, a city that had been peacefully surrendered, is as well documented as anything in history. You can prove it by Northern letters, diaries, and newspapers without touching a single Southern source. This work has been re-published under the title *A City Laid Waste* with a good introduction by Simms scholar David Aiken.

43.

Nashville 1864: The Dying of the Light

By Madison Jones

The celebrated Agrarian novelist Madison Jones pictures the somber waning days of the Southern Confederacy through the experiences of a boy witness to the battlefield. We feel the sad experience of people fighting bravely in a losing cause.

44.

The Illustrated Confederate Reader

Edited by Rod Gragg

South Carolinian Rod Gragg has published over 20 books of American history, on the War Between the States, the colonial period, World War II, and other subjects. He is an outstanding "nonprofessional" historian, and I mean that as a high compliment. There are many Confederate readers —collections of memoirs and documents that illustrate the experiences of Southerners in the war. Some are very good, but this is the best I have ever encountered. A beautiful collection of personal experiences and eyewitness accounts that illustrate the devotion, heroism and sacrifice of Southerners, both soldiers and civilians, in their lost war for independence. Here are a few more very good collections of real, first-hand Confederate experiences: Walter Sullivan, *The War the Women Lived*; Daniel W. Barefoot, *Let Us Die Like Brave Men*; Lee Jacobs, *Deo Vindice: Heroes in Gray Forever*.

45.

Shadows of Blue and Grey: The Civil War Writings of Ambrose Bierce
Edited by Brian M. Thomsen

Ambrose Bierce was a Midwesterner and a hard-fighting volunteer Union soldier from the first to the last of the War Between the States. After the war he became a popular if somewhat cynical author and journalist whose collected works filled 12 volumes. In 1914, in his seventies, he disappeared forever during a revolution in Mexico. Why cite Bierce as an entry in our guide to The War? Because Bierce was an honest man who respected valiant foes and an honourable people. Once, when the remains of an unburied Confederate soldier were found in his vicinity, he declared that he was going there and apologise. He savaged the Republicans who tried to prevent Confederate soldiers from being remembered and honoured, and made fun of mediocre political soldiers like Garfield who the Republican press promoted into heroes. When he was captured, he liked his gentlemanly Southern captors far better than the "mongrel foreigners" who were his fellow soldiers. After the war he helped Southerners hide their cotton from crooked federal agents. In one of his recollections he tells how his division commander was surreptitiously published by Sherman for trying to put out the Columbia fires. The book includes both fiction and non-fiction writings that were never previously collected.

II.

NOT "ABOUT SLAVERY"

BECAUSE OF AMERICANS' PREOCCUPATION with race and victimhood, and because a belief in the righteousness of the war against the South is essential to American self-love, it is now declared at every level that the War was "about slavery," that is, primarily fought for emancipation and against evil defenders of enslavement. In simple fact, as Frederick Douglass pointed out, never at any time was the North's primary concern the condition or fate of African Americans, who suffered greatly from the U.S. invasion of their homeland and were left in many respects worse off than they had been. The war of conquest against the South was carried out so that the ruling elements of the North could retain economic and political control of Southern territory, resources and people. That is not a Southern accusation —it is evident in the words of Northerners themselves. It was quite blatant in speeches, sermons, editorials, and letters. Any thorough examination of Northern rhetoric about the war will find every characteristic of *imperialism.*

The fate of African Americans was incidental to the Northern war effort. The general Northern attitude toward African Americans was that they were a blight that must be kept in the South. Lincoln and Northern newspapers declared openly for war on grounds that their prosperity could not stand the lack of the South's exports and tariff payments. Senator John Sherman of Ohio, Radical Republican and brother of General Sherman, declared that establishing a national banking system was a more important goal than freeing the slaves.

In fairly recent times, serious historians have begun to look closely at the North. Their discoveries have provided a long missing perspective on the central event of American history. Most of these historians, it should be stressed, are not pro-Confederate.

46.

When in the Course of Human Events: Arguing the Case for Southern Secession

By Charles Adams

Californian Charles Adams, a learned historian of taxation, makes the full case that the War Between the States was a matter of economics. The North was not interested in slavery but in preserving its economic domination by which was extracted much of the wealth of the South for the benefit of the Northern moneyed class. Adams marshals heavy evidence supporting the idea that the war was brought on and cruelly and illegally waged by the Northern government for motives that were far from righteous. Correspondingly, the honourable South, which only wanted to be left alone, suffered greatly for defending itself. Adams strengthened his case by a subsequent edited collection, *Slavery, Secession, and Civil War: Views from the United Kingdom and Europe, 1856—1865.* The observations of European commentators and newspapers, free from the impulse to promote Northern righteousness, are very illuminating. Charles Dickens: "The Northern onslaught upon slavery was no more than a piece of specious humbug designed to conceal its desire for economic control of the Southern states."

47.

Punished with Poverty, The Suffering South: Prosperity to Poverty and the Continuing Struggle

By James Ronald Kennedy & Walter Donald Kennedy

"It is true we are completely under the saddle of Massachusetts and Connecticut," wrote Tomas Jefferson in 1798, "and that they ride us very hard, cruelly insulting our feelings, as well as exhausting our strength and substance." Jefferson was asking whether joining New England in a Union had not become a bad bargain for the South. Through the colonial period and into the early 19th century, the South was almost fantastically prosperous. Since then, with tariffs and North-favouring expenditures, destruction by invasion, Reconstruction looting, and partial legislation, Southerners, black and white, have been, and still are, up to the present moment, the poorest Americans —and Southern "feelings" suffer from constant denunciation for being out-of-step in religion and values from the rest of the U.S. The Kennedy brothers, long known as fearless spokesman for the Southern people, have written an original and important contribution to Southern history. They relate the long story of the poverty *imposed* on the South. They wonder why Southerners are not more conscious of their inferior position in "America," and they propose unconventional political action to do something about it. *Punished with Poverty* is followed by *Dixie Rising*, a handbook for that political action.

48.

Trading with the Enemy: The Covert Economy During the American Civil War
By Philip Leigh

One of the most independent-minded and thorough among recent American historians, Leigh brings to light a neglected aspect of the war. It is largely the story of how Northern greed dominated the war against the South, in particular in regard to the seizure of cotton, the most valuable commodity in America. Lincoln and his minions were deeply involved in activities that enriched a few but that actually harmed the effort of the boys in blue. Another example of Leigh's outstanding work on the war is *The Confederacy at Flood Tide*.

49.

Clash of Extremes: The Economic Origins of the Civil War

By Marc Egnal

Though by no means a sympathiser with the South, Egnal has looked afresh at the case for economics as the cause of the War. The meat of the book is his description of the Great Lakes industrial empire that appeared in the 1850s —Cleveland, Detroit, Chicago. This new force was determined to build a world-class economy with government favour and subsidy, and of course, riches for the well-placed. The appearance of this new force (which Lincoln represented) was the game changer. It brought the shift of the Midwest economic and political focus from the South to the East and a determination to overcome contrary Southern interests and Constitutional scruples.

50.

And a Few More

"Mainstream" historians in recent times have not seriously considered the case for the North's primary economic motivation for the war, assuming that recent writers who favour that interpretation are not sufficiently enraged over slavery. Yet the case has a long and respectable tradition going back at least to one of the greatest American historians, Charles A. Beard. Books touching on the North's economic and other non-slavery motives for the War: Charles A. and Mary R. Beard, *The Rise of American Civilization*; Richard F. Bensel, *Yankee Leviathan*; Leonard P. Curry, *Blueprint for Modern America: Non-Military Legislation of the First Civil War Congress*; Thomas DiLorenzo, *Hamilton's Curse*; Thomas Fleming, *A Disease in the Public Mind*; Susan-Mary Grant, *North Over South: Northern Nationalism and American History in the Antebellum Era*; James and Walter Kennedy, *Yankee Empire: Aggressive Abroad and Despotic at Home*; Heather Cox Richardson, *"The Greatest Nation on Earth": Republican Economic Policies During the Civil War*; Frank van der Linden, *The Dark Intrigue: The True Story of a Civil War Conspiracy*; and *North Against South* by Ludwell H. Johnson (No. 2 above) Similar truths are presented in some of the titles below regarding Lincoln. There is also much relevant material in Volume 3 of Allan Nevins's standard history, *The War for the Union.*

III.

LINCOLN WORSHIP: THE CURE

51.

The Real Lincoln: A New Look at Abraham Lincoln, His Agenda, and an Unnecessary War

By Thomas J. DiLorenzo

Here is rendered inimitably Lincoln, the canny corporate lawyer, crafty self-seeking politician, agent of crony capitalism, and white supremacist. DiLorenzo, an economic historian, approaches the subject with plenty of evidence of the clay feet of America's greatest hero. Who knows what good the truth can do —Lincoln worship is not a matter of reason but of mysticism. DiLorenzo followed up this best-seller with *Lincoln Unmasked: What You're Not Supposed to Know about Dishonest Abe.* In that book DiLorenzo expertly skewers the "historians" of the Lincoln cult and provides an amusing account of all the pretty sayings that over a long period have been falsely attributed to Lincoln.

52.

Lincoln —The Man (1931)

by Edgar Lee Masters

Masters (1868—1950) holds a permanent place in American poetry for his *Spoon River Anthology.* Two factors make his study of Lincoln of great interest. First, he grew up and lived most of his life in the Lincoln neighbourhood, not far from Springfield, Illinois, and thus had access to much unwritten lore. Second, he was a practicing lawyer much involved in fighting against the corruptions of the Republican party and Big Business that dominated his State. So he had a good grasp of Lincoln as primarily a tool of Northern capitalism, guilty of a horrible war, and the father of a regime of evil oppressions of the common folk. The book, which ought to be read by every Lincoln admirer (but, of course, won't be) was republished in a good edition in 1997.

53.
Lincoln As He Really Was
By Charles T. Pace

With much previously unnoticed information, the author traces the life and character of Lincoln closely and in an original way. Lincoln's life, as we see by chapter and verse, was that of a pathologically ambitious, self-centered, disingenuous, and cynical power-seeker who brought immeasurable destruction upon his country.

54.

Northern Opposition to Mr. Lincoln's War

Edited by D. Jonathan White

One of the best kept secrets of American history is the great number, patriotism, wisdom, and respectability of Northerners who opposed Lincoln's war of conquest against the Southern people. In 1864 over 1,800,000 votes were cast against Lincoln (45%) despite the fact the soldiers with bayonets and Republican mobs kept many anti-Lincoln voters from the polls. This work presents nine articles that begin a serious look at Lincoln's Northern opposition, though it is only the beginning of exploration of a vast subject. A group historians, including Marshall DeRosa, Richard M. Gamble, John Chodes, Joseph Stromberg, Brion McClanahan, and others, look at the brave editors, clergymen, descendants of Founding Fathers, disillusioned and disgusted soldiers, and others who suffered, sometimes with life-threatening severity, for their stands. So much strong opposition is really not surprising when acceptance of the truth of the Southern Constitutional position was still widespread in the North, when many Northerners realised that the real Republican agenda was exploitive control of the economy and that Lincoln was doing great damage to the Constitution and American freedom. On the same subject, the historian Frank Klement published a number of informative books about the so-called "Copperheads" in the Midwest that are now forgotten but are worth a look. See also Robert S. Harper, *Lincoln and the Press*, and *Lincoln's Wrath* by Jeffrey Manber and Neil Dahlstom, which document Lincoln's prewar and wartime manipulation and coercion of the press.

55.

Why Was Lincoln Murdered?

By Otto Eisenschiml

We will never know the truth of Lincoln's assassination. That is because the investigation was controlled by Edwin M. Stanton, a man of well-documented duplicity. Stanton, the Union's Secretary of War, was the closest thing to a Heinrich Himmler who ever held high office in the U.S. As always with high profile assassinations, theories have flourished that question the official story. Why was Booth, cornered and injured, killed rather than captured and questioned? Why were pages torn from his diary before it was seen by more than a few? Why did Booth's body not receive any independent identification? What is the significance of Booth's meeting with certain wealthy Northerners in Montreal not long before the assassination? Why were the "conspirators," including Mrs. Surratt, held incommunicado in brutal confinement and quickly executed? Most importantly, who gained the most profit from the assassination? The answer to that is clear —the Radical Republicans who anticipated that Lincoln would be too easy on "Reconstruction." Eisenshciml was an Austrian-born scientist who did extensive serious research and published much on the War Between the States. He argues that Lincoln was the victim of a conspiracy engineered by Stanton and other Radical Republicans, and presents a good deal of evidence. His book, published in 1937, has produced much response, pro and con, up to the present. Perhaps the most important thing about this book is what it reveals about the evil character of the people who controlled the U.S. during and after The War. I can also recommend *Mary Surratt: An American Tragedy* by Elizabeth Steger Trindal, and *The Dark Intrigue: The True Story of a Civil War Conspiracy* by Frank van der Linden.

56.
American Terrorists: Lincoln's Armies in the South
By Michael Andrew Grissom

Oklahoman Grissom, author of *Southern by the Grace of God* and other popular books, has made a strong addition to the literature of Yankee atrocities against Southern women and children. He includes hard-hitting material from every State. In a similar vein I can recommend *Blood and War at My Doorstep: North Carolina Civilians in the War*

Between the States by Brenda Chambers McKean, and *South Carolina Civilians in Sherman's Path* by Karen Stokes. Lincoln, of course, has the ultimate responsibility for total war against the women and children of the South.

57.

Emancipation Hell: The Tragedy Wrought by Lincoln's Emancipation Proclamation

By Kirkpatrick Sale

Kirkpatrick Sale, Vermont patriot and author of the devolution classic *Human Scale*, addresses his independent mind to the emancipation of Southern slaves by Northern power. He casts this supposedly glorious part of American history in a realistic and critical light. Emancipation, yes. But as a military measure during a cruel war of invasion and indifferent to any provision for the place of the emancipated in American society? An emancipation that the leading African American spokesman of the 19th century, Frederick Douglass, denounced as a tragedy that left black Americans "worse off in many respects than" under slavery? This is an essential contribution to the needed duty of Americans to understand their real rather than their fictional and self-righteous history. Henri Narceise, former slave of

Mississippi: "Dey went and turned us loose like a passel of cattle, and didn't show us nothin' or give us nothin'."

5 8.

Mr. Lincoln Goes to War

by William Marvel

Until Americans get a realistic grasp of Lincoln, they will remain in a distorted orientation toward the world that justifies our present delusional global empire. Like Lincoln's crusade, it is a compound of greed and a presumptuous false morality of "the greatest nation on earth" with the mission of correcting the evils of other peoples. An interesting recent attempt at Lincolnian realism is the four volumes of William Marvel's *Mr. Lincoln Goes to War*. Marvel is no friend of the South, but he has done genuine research in the primary sources and demonstrates the negatives, ambiguity and compromises of Lincoln's crusade. *Mr. Lincoln Goes to War* is followed by *Lincoln's Darkest Year: The War in 1862; The Great Task Remaining: The Third Year of Lincoln's War*; and *Tarnished Victory: Finishing Lincoln's War*. Interestingly, in his brief comments about Reconstruction Marvel follows the current "mainstream" line. If he does the kind of deep research on Reconstruction that he has done on the war, he will become a revisionist on that subject also.

Sick from Freedom: African-American Illness and Suffering During the Civil War and Reconstruction

By Jim Downs

This recent work (2012) by a medical historian gives a grim report on what actually happened to black Southerners as they were "emancipated" by the boys in blue. What happened was a catastrophe of abuse, sickness, disease, suffering, and death. These facts need to be faced by the glorifiers of Lincoln. Several recent historians have been upgrading previous estimates of Southern civilian deaths, black and white, resulting from Lincoln's invasion.

60.

"Searching for Lincoln: A Documentary Film" (2015)

We close with a remarkable documentary from Darlin Productions that examines Lincoln candidly from many different angles. A must see.

AFTERWORD

THE GREAT SOUTHERN SCHOLARS M.E. Bradford and Thomas H. Landess planned a book on Lincoln and his egregious legacy that was never completed. But portions have been published. There are seven relevant pieces in *Life, Literature and Lincoln: A Tom Landess Reader.* Bradford's ground-breaking essays on Lincoln's legacy of "continuing revolution" and his "language of hate and fear" are scattered in his *A Better Guide than Reason, The Reactionary Imperative,* and *Against the Barbarians.*

I declined to include the works of Edward A. Pollard, *Southern History of the War* and *The Lost Cause,* among essential books on The War, although they contain a great deal of useful material about Yankee misbehaviour and Southern soldiers' many victories against superior numbers. (I prefer the former because much of it was written with immediacy during the war.) Pollard thought Confederate leaders and people should have resorted to all-out revolutionary war and was a relentless enemy of Jefferson Davis and the Confederate government, which he blamed for defeat. For better or worse, Southern leaders and people were fighting a protective and preservative war and could not adopt Pollard's revolutionary posture without a change in character.

ABOUT THE AUTHOR

DR. CLYDE N. WILSON is Emeritus Distinguished Professor of History of the University of South Carolina, where he served from 1971 to 2006. He holds a Ph.D. from the University of North Carolina at Chapel Hill. Wilson was editor of the 28-volume edition of *The Papers of John C. Calhoun* which has received high praise. He is author or editor of more than 20 other books and over 700 articles, essays, and reviews in a variety of books and journals, and has lectured all over the U.S. and in Europe.

Dr. Wilson directed 17 doctoral dissertations, a number of which have been published. His books written or edited include *Why the South Will Survive, Carolina Cavalier: The Life and Mind of James Johnston Pettigrew, The Essential Calhoun,* three volumes of *The Dictionary of Literary Biography* on American Historians, *From Union to Empire: Essays in the Jeffersonian Tradition, Defending Dixie: Essays in Southern History and Culture, Chronicles of the South,* and *The Yankee Problem.*

Dr. Wilson is founding director of the Society of Independent Southern Historians; former president of the St. George Tucker Society for Southern Studies; recipient of the Bostick Prize for Contributions to South Carolina Letters, the first annual John Randolph Society

Lifetime Achievement Award, and of the Robert E. Lee Medal of the Sons of Confederate Veterans. He is M.E. Bradford Distinguished Professor of the Abbeville Institute; Contributing Editor of *Chronicles: A Magazine of American Culture*; founding dean of the Stephen D. Lee Institute, educational arm of the Sons of Confederate Veterans; and co-founder of Shotwell Publishing.

Dr. Wilson has two grown daughters, an excellent son-in-law, and two outstanding grandsons. He lives in the Dutch Fork of South Carolina, not far from the Santee Swamp where Francis Marion and his men rested between raids on the first invader.

AVAILABLE FROM SHOTWELL PUBLISHING

IF YOU ENJOYED THIS BOOK, perhaps some of our other titles will pique your interest. The following titles are currently available (or will be shortly) from Shotwell at Amazon and all major online book retailers.

JOYCE BENNETT

+ *Maryland, My Maryland: The Cultural Cleansing of a Small Southern State*

JERRY BREWER

+ *Dismantling the Republic*

ANDREW P. CALHOUN, JR.

+ *My Own Darling Wife: Letters From a Confederate Volunteer [John Francis Calhoun]*

JOHN CHODES

+ *Segregation: Federal Policy or Racism?*
+ *Washington's KKK: The Union League During Southern Reconstruction*

PAUL C. GRAHAM

- *Confederaphobia: An American Epidemic*
- *When the Yankees Come: Former South Carolina Slaves Remember Sherman's Invasion (Voices from the Dust I)*

JOSEPH JAY

- *Sacred Conviction: The South's Stand for Biblical Authority*

JAMES R. KENNEDY

- *Dixie Rising: Rules for Rebels*

JAMES R. & WALTER D. KENNEDY

- *Punished with Poverty: The Suffering South*
- *Yankee Empire: Aggressive Abroad and Despotic At Home*

PHILIP LEIGH

- *The Devil's Town: Hot Spring During the Gangster Era*

MICHAEL MARTIN

- *Southern Grit: Sensing the Siege at Petersburg*

LEWIS LIBERMAN

- *Snowflake Buddies: ABCs for Leftism for Kids!*

CHARLES T. PACE

- *Lincoln As He Really Was*
- *Southern Independence. Why War?*

JAMES RUTLEDGE ROESCH

- *From Founding Fathers to Fire Eaters: The Constitutional Doctrine of States' Rights in the Old South*

KIRKPATRICK SALE

- *Emancipation Hell: The Tragedy Wrought By Lincoln's Emancipation Proclamation*

KAREN STOKES

- *A Legion of Devils: Sherman in South Carolina*
- *Carolina Love Letters*

JOHN VINSON

- *Southerner, Take Your Stand!*

HOWARD RAY WHITE

- *Understanding Creation and Evolution*

WALTER KIRK WOOD

- *Beyond Slavery: The Northern Romantic Nationalist Origins of America's Civil War*

CLYDE N. WILSON

- *Annals of the Stupid Party: Republicans Before Trump (The Wilson Files 3)*
- *Lies My Teacher Told Me: The True History of the War for Southern Independence*
- *Nullification: Reclaiming Consent of the Governed (The Wilson Files 2)*
- *The Old South: 50 Essential Books (Southern Reader's Guide I)*
- *The War Between the States: 60 Essential Books (Southern Reader's Guide II)*
- *The Yankee Problem: An American Dilemma (The Wilson Files 1)*

GREEN ALTAR BOOKS (Literary Imprint)

RANDALL IVEY

- *A New England Romance & Other SOUTHERN Stories*

JAMES EVERETT KIBLER

- *Tiller (Clay Bank County, IV)*

KAREN STOKES

- *Belles: A Carolina Romance*
- *Honor in the Dust*
- *The Immortals*
- *The Soldier's Ghost: A Tale of Charleston*

_____

GOLD-BUG (Mystery & Suspense Imprint)

MICHAEL ANDREW GRISSOM

- *Billie Jo*

BRANDI PERRY

- *Splintered: A New Orleans Tale*

MARTIN L. WILSON

- *To Jekyll and Hide*

FREE BOOK OFFER

Sign-up for new release notification and receive a **FREE** downloadable edition of *Lies My Teacher Told Me: The True History of the War for Southern Independence* by Dr. Clyde N. Wilson by visiting FreeLiesBook.com or by texting the word "Dixie" to 345345. You can always unsubscribe and keep the book, so you've got nothing to lose!

SOUTHERN WITHOUT APOLOGY.